THE COOPERATIVE LEARNING COMPANION

by Terri Breeden
and
Janice Mosley

Incentive Publications, Inc.
Nashville, Tennessee

Illustrated by Kathleen Bullock
Cover by Geoffrey Brittingham
Edited by Jan Keeling

ISBN 0-86530-239-1

Table of Contents

ABOUT THIS BOOK

The Cooperative Learning Companion is a supplemental resource to use in your cooperative classroom. Two teachers who use Cooperative Learning in their classrooms wrote this book with you in mind. We hope you find this book helpful, practical, teacher-friendly, and simple. In these pages you will find:

- Answers to questions most often asked about Cooperative Learning
- Ideas for teaching cooperative skills
- Quick cooperative ideas
- Forms
- Letters
- Rewards
- Bulletin board suggestions
- Lesson plan guides
- And more!

When it comes to Cooperative Learning, this book could prove to be your life saver. Just remember this slogan:

Sink or swim, we are all in this together!

MOST-OFTEN-ASKED QUESTIONS

This chapter is devoted to the questions that seem to come up most often when teaching Cooperative Learning workshops. Skim through the next few pages to find the questions that most often arise in *your* mind.

1. What is a quick definition of Cooperative Learning?

Cooperative Learning: Students working together in structured groups, helping each other learn, and earning rewards for their efforts.

2. How is Cooperative Learning different from "group work"?

There are two major differences. First, Cooperative Learning groups have a definite structure, with students of various achievement levels grouped together by the teacher. Second, group interdependence must be fostered. (Group interdependence occurs when students realize that it takes all members of a group working together to achieve a goal.)

3. Why is Cooperative Learning receiving so much attention?

In a study of people who had been fired from their jobs, researchers found that 90% of the respondents were not fired as a result of poor job performance. The firings were due to poor job attitudes, interpersonal relationships, and inappropriate behavior. It has become clear that cooperation is imperative for those who want to achieve success in life, and the skills associated with cooperation are easily taught in a Cooperative Learning classroom. The educational community should be as concerned about teaching a child social skills as it is about teaching a child mathematics.

4. "Interdependence" is a word associated with cooperative groups. Define it for me.

A real world example of interdependence is what happens during a football game. The quarterback cannot possibly score a touchdown without the help of his teammates. He must have the receiver to catch the ball. And one cannot discount the offensive players' role in holding back the other team. In a Cooperative Learning group, one student may be filling out a worksheet while another checks the answers and a third explains the concept. The goal—learning—is achieved by all. That is interdependence!

5. What is the best size for a cooperative group?

According to most of the research, cooperative groups should consist of two to six students. Primary students seem to function better in smaller groups. (Smaller groups are also easier for the teacher who is new at Cooperative Learning.) A teacher must consider the ages of the students, the size of the class, the availability of equipment/supplies, attendance, racial make-up of the class, room arrangements, and type of activity when determining group sizes.

6. Speaking as a classroom teacher, what advantages do you see in Cooperative Learning?

The most important change we have seen as a result of Cooperative Learning is more positive peer interaction. Students have crossed racial and gender lines in friendship choices. They also show more appreciation for one another's opinions. Other positive results have been:

- There are fewer papers to grade when a teacher assigns a consensus paper.

- When a question arises, the teacher can explain the answer to a group of children, rather than to an individual student.

- The students enjoy working with classmates.

- The students can explain material to their classmates in "kid language." (Never underestimate this ability!)

- The students assume responsibility for learning.

- The students assume a more active role in the learning environment because each child is assigned a job.

7. How often do you use Cooperative Learning methods?

Let us remember that Cooperative Learning is just one of several methods used in a classroom. Cooperative Learning is used whenever the teacher believes that a cooperative lesson would be the best way to achieve a particular objective.

But most people want a more concrete answer to this question: Generally speaking, we find we use Cooperative Learning once a week. Sometimes, we may use a cooperative activity that takes up several class periods for several days. At other times, we may not use a cooperative activity for two weeks. Remember, Cooperative Learning is a tool for the teacher. Find a schedule that fits you and your students.

Most-Often-Asked Questions

8. How do I decide which students will form a group? Is homogeneous or heterogeneous grouping better?

Homogeneous groups can be used occasionally, but heterogeneous groups should be used for most activities. The rule of thumb is to place a high achiever, a low achiever, and a middle achiever in each group. If larger groups are desired, just try to keep a mix of abilities. It is also desirable to mix students by gender and race.

9. How do I decide who is a high, middle, or low student?

A teacher needs to find a numerical grade that is reflective of the student's ability. This score will serve as a base score. (See *The Middle Grades Teacher's Handbook For Cooperative Learning*, Incentive Publications, pp. 12–14, for more information.)

10. In the lower grades, or for special education classes, we do not give numerical grades. What should I do?

Teachers know their students and have good instincts. Choose criteria that fit your students. You may wish to establish a color code.

11. How do I arrange cooperative groups if I teach more than one subject? Do I change my groups for each discipline?

It is true that a student who is a high achiever in math may not be a high achiever in English. How can a teacher organize groups if he or she teaches both subjects? If the teacher who is new at Cooperative Learning were to attempt to organize different cooperative groups for each subject, he or she might be overwhelmed. The best advice we can give is to arrive at an average base score for each student. For example, a student who has a 98 average in math and a 78 in English will have an average base score of 88.

12. How often do you change groups?

There is no right or wrong answer to this question. Some teachers keep the groups together for an entire semester. Other groups stay together only during a particular unit. Most schools are set up around six- or nine-week periods, and it is best to change groups at the end of a period. By changing groups, students will get to work with more class members, and they will also benefit from being assigned a different role in the group.

13. What roles do I assign?

The roles that are suggested in Cooperative Learning books are only suggestions. The point of roles is that each student needs to have a specific job to perform. A specific role helps a student understand his or her job. Role suggestions include Runner, Checker, Encourager, Recorder, Reader, Timekeeper, Materials Manager, and Sergeant-At-Arms.

14. How often do you change base scores?

The base score can change only when you rearrange the groups.

15. Do the students ever get to pick their own groups?

No. If you let students pick their groups, they will not branch out of their known peer groups. Remember, one of the differences between cooperative groups and just "groups" is the structure that the teacher gives to the group by crossing racial and ability lines.

16. Do you ever grade cooperative work?

Yes, almost all of the time. The teacher should be trying to establish the feeling of interdependence, and a group grade is a good way to let a group of four students know they are not just four separate individuals. They sink or swim together. Generally speaking, cooperative work is very good because students have put their heads together to complete the work, another student has checked all the answers, and the teacher has been nearby to help.

17. I can see how Cooperative Learning helps the lower- and middle-achieving child, but how does it help the high achiever?

The high-achieving student does benefit. Very rarely does even the high achiever understand every assignment given by a teacher. If he or she does have a weak area, the other members can help. If the high achiever does understand the material, the opportunity to teach other members helps the high-achieving student retain his or her knowledge. Finally, the social skills training is invaluable for anyone in the group. Even high-achieving students need to learn cooperative skills.

18. What do you do if a group member is absent?

The same thing that adults do when a committee member is not present: Carry on!

19. What do you do if one child is doing all the work?

There are several ways to handle this problem. At first, the teacher may just have to remind the group that every member has a role and must do her own job. If this does not help, the next intervention might be to have all group members place their pencils in the center of the table. When a student does part of the activity, he removes the pencil. Then he cannot participate again until all the pencils are removed from the table. For more information about possible cooperative behavior problems, see *The Middle Grades Teacher's Handbook For Cooperative Learning,* Incentive Publications, page 21.

20. How do you discipline the class during cooperative group time?

The teacher must clearly and specifically discuss cooperative group behavior before students engage in a cooperative activity. Post three to five cooperative group rules in the classroom. Enforce the rules as you normally do with other rules. It is also wise to spend time helping students learn cooperative norms of behavior before beginning formal cooperative groups.

21. I don't understand how the point system works.

The point system is based on the idea that students can earn points for IMPROVEMENT. A child who scores 10 points above his base score can earn as many points as a student who receives a 100. On page 60 you will find a detailed review of this element of cooperative learning.

22. How and when do you reward cooperative groups?

Informally, cooperative groups should be rewarded any time they follow cooperative norms of behavior. Verbal praise is quite appropriate to use while circulating around the classroom. Use phrases like, "Group four is excellent at keeping their voices low," or "I really like how the members of group three are all doing their part of the project." This positive reinforcement is critical to the success of a cooperative classroom. You may formally reward cooperative groups either at the end of an assignment or before cooperative groups are "changed." Rewards may be cooperative group points, homework passes, certificates, or candy.

23. What if a cooperative group argues all the time?

Some disagreement should be expected. The students may be upset if they are not grouped with their friends. The teacher's first intervention should be to let it be known that no one will be moved from the group. This helps the students to realize that they are going to have to get past their initial disappointment with the group. Remind the students that they are going to receive grades on cooperative work, so it would be wise to try to work on the assignment. The teacher may also state that students may argue only about academic problems, and that personalities must be left out of the discussion. If the problem persists, the teacher may choose to assign the job of Mediator to one students. If the conflict is too large for a student to handle, the teacher may need to "conference" with the group. Only in extreme cases should group members be removed or added to a group.

24. What do I do if one student refuses to work with the group? Several members of the group work together while one student does his work alone.

One easy way to deal with this problem is by using the consensus assignment. Only one paper is accepted from the group. All members must sign their names at the top of the paper. If another paper is turned in for a grade, it is returned to the group ungraded.

25. What do I tell my students' parents about Cooperative Learning?

On pages 62 and 63 are sample letters that may be sent home to parents. Most parents see no problem with Cooperative Learning. If a parent strongly objects to cooperative grades, the cooperative grades can be omitted when averaging the student's grades. Research has shown that cooperative grades do raise a student's average.

26. How do you teach cooperative skills?

The answer to this question may be found on many of the pages of this book. Several sample lessons are included to give the teacher an idea of how cooperative skills may be taught.

27. Do I have to throw out my old lesson plans?

The typical teacher has spent years developing fabulous lessons, and it would be a crime to discard them. It is important to keep in mind that Cooperative Learning is only one method that may be used in the classroom. Therefore, some of those old lessons can be used in exactly the same fashion as before. It is also helpful to use old lessons as springboards for new and exciting cooperative lessons. On page 72 of this book you will find a sample cooperative lesson plan guide that will help you convert your old lessons to cooperative lessons. *(The Middle Grades Teacher's Handbook For Cooperative Learning* also includes "Blue Print" pages that instruct a teacher how to utilize the textbook and former lesson plans into cooperative lessons.)

28. How do I write a cooperative lesson?

There are two main concepts to keep in mind. The lesson must be structured so that interdependence can be achieved. And it is important that each group member is able to contribute to the lesson. (Ask yourself: how can this lesson be structured around group roles?)

29. How can I use my textbook in cooperative groups?

The textbook can be a gold mine for cooperative activities. Many textbook publishers are even now including cooperative activities in the teacher's editions. In a math textbook, the odd problems can be assigned to the group, with individual followup assignment of the even problems for homework. In social studies, a chapter review can be done cooperatively, while the chapter test is the individual assignment. In science, experiments are ideal cooperative assignments if the teacher assigns appropriate roles. In language arts, groups can be assigned almost any exercise found in the text.

30. The class seems to get out of control during cooperative learning. What do you suggest can be done?

Reinforcement of cooperative group rules is critical. One rule that really helps to control behavior is that students must stay in their groups. There should be no wandering around the room. Another option is to complete a Teacher Observation Form (page 64). Pick a cooperative skill your class is having trouble with and walk around the room taking data on the groups. "Using quiet voices" is a great skill to reinforce when the object is to get control of the class.

*31. Since I have implemented Cooperative Learning, I have noticed a lot more talking during **individual** assignments. What should I do?*

This is a common side effect of Cooperative Learning! The best advice is to make a clear distinction between cooperative groups and individual assignments.

32. I teach Special Education. Can I use cooperative groups?

Yes, with some modifications. It would be best to keep the groups small. The Special Education teacher may have to spend more time teaching cooperative skills to the class. It would also be wise to delay the implementation of Cooperative Learning until the strengths and weaknesses of the class are clearly identified. It is critical that the basic classroom structure be left intact as much as possible. Short cooperative lessons are best. Group processing is an extremely important aspect of the Special Education cooperative classroom, and students' roles must be clearly defined.

33. I have several learning-disabled students in my class. Can they do cooperative group work?

Yes, Cooperative Learning allows Special and Regular Education students to work hand-in-hand. Often Cooperative Learning can really help a child's self-esteem. The teacher must carefully place a mainstreamed child into a group. Some preparation needs to be done before the cooperative activity is assigned. Perhaps the resource teacher or a high-achieving student could do a similar activity with the learning-disabled student before the cooperative activity.

34. Doesn't Cooperative Learning take a lot of the teacher's time?

Cooperative Learning can be very time-consuming. Its initial planning usually takes a bit more time than you may be used to. Students can be very helpful in organizing materials and making bulletin boards. And this book provides many companion materials that will save you time and help you organize quickly.

BUILDING A FOUNDATION FOR COOPERATIVE SKILLS

BLUE-PRINT FOR SUCCESS

1. INSTRUCTION - TEACHER DIRECTED

| CLASSROOM DISPLAYS | VALIDATION | VIGNETTES |

2. STUDENT UNDERSTANDING

| T-CHARTS | PHRASES | MODELING |

3. PRACTICE

| STUDENT ROLES | OBSERVATION | REWARD |

4. PROCESSING

| GROUP REPORTS | DISCUSSIONS | FEEDBACK |

5. COOPERATIVE SKILLS — MAINTENANCE

BUILDING A FOUNDATION FOR COOPERATIVE SKILLS

Before the advent of Cooperative Learning, students were taught to keep their eyes on their own papers, to be responsible for their own grades, and to refrain from sharing homework. Therefore, teachers who want their students to learn *cooperative* skills must spend a little time helping their students "unlearn" some individualized, competitive habits they have acquired.

Cooperative skills are numerous. Those that come naturally to the student do not, of course, need to be formally taught. Some of the skills can be learned simply through the enforcement of Cooperative Classroom rules. A number of cooperative skills may, however, need special attention.

The classroom teacher has many academic objectives to meet during the school year, and will not be able to allot tremendous amounts of time to the teaching of cooperative skills. Teachers will have to determine for themselves how much time they can spare to fine-tune students' cooperative skills.

A plan for teaching cooperative skills is illustrated by the model on page 20. It is wise to work on one cooperative skill at a time. Try to determine your students' cooperative deficits. This will help you in your selection of skills to emphasize. A list of cooperative skills includes:

- Using quiet voices
- Explaining answers
- Summarizing
- Listening
- Giving directions
- Encouraging participation
- Criticizing ideas, not people
- Expressing support
- Expressing feelings
- Asking probing questions

When working on a cooperative skill, some kind of teacher-directed INSTRUCTION must be given first. The teacher may choose to post a definition of the skill, use banners and posters, create a bulletin board, tell a story (vignette), or give a short lecture on how the skill is useful in cooperative groups and in life. The teacher can validate the importance of the skill by emphasizing that cooperative points or other types of rewards will be given when the skill is demonstrated.

BUILDING A FOUNDATION FOR COOPERATIVE SKILLS

The teacher may check for UNDERSTANDING of the skill by asking students to think of a phrase that would help them to remember the skill. You may have the students fill out a T-Chart such as the one on page 34 for "Constructive Criticism," or ask a class member to perform a brief modeling exercise.

PRACTICE makes perfect when it comes to Cooperative Learning! A cooperative skill can be clarified by breaking it down into specific components. Teachers or students may spend some time in formal observation of the groups, on the lookout for demonstrated cooperative skills. Rewards or verbal praise may be used as a reinforcement for students who are demonstrating the skill.

PROCESSING is essential in the acquisition of a skill. A formal group processing worksheet may be given to the class. Or, after observation of groups, a class discussion may be held to give an opportunity for feedback on what was observed. This feedback can be a great help in making students aware of how they are doing.

A cooperative group MAINTENANCE schedule should be implemented to ensure that the groups continue to use previously-learned skills. The maintenance may be in the form of a "pop observation," or simple ongoing verbal praise may keep the skill reinforced in the students' minds.

We strongly urge that the teaching of skills be employed in cooperative settings. Initially, a teacher may wish to divide the class into groups of two for practice of a particular skill. Later the cooperative skill may be integrated into another cooperative lesson. Cooperative skill training can occur at any time during the conducting of a cooperative lesson.

On page 23 you will find a Cooperative Skill Plan Sheet that can serve as a guide when the teacher is developing original lesson plans. On this sheet are listed the five phases of cooperative skill acquisition. Page 24 shows a sample bulletin board which may be used during instruction of cooperative skills.

We have included ten sample cooperative skill lessons on pages 25–50. These demonstrate various approaches to show the diversity that can be incorporated into cooperative skill training. Two guiding principles of cooperative skill lesson planning: 1. Include all five phases of the model. 2. Keep the lessons simple enough to be able to complete in a brief period of time.

BUILDING A FOUNDATION FOR COOPERATIVE SKILLS

COOPERATIVE SKILL PLAN SHEET

Cooperative Skill _____

Instruction Phase _____
_____
_____
_____
_____

Student Understanding Phase _____
_____
_____
_____
_____
_____
_____
_____
_____
_____

Practice Phase _____
_____
_____
_____
_____

Processing Phase _____
_____
_____
_____

Maintenance Phase _____
_____
_____
_____

BUILDING A FOUNDATION FOR COOPERATIVE SKILLS

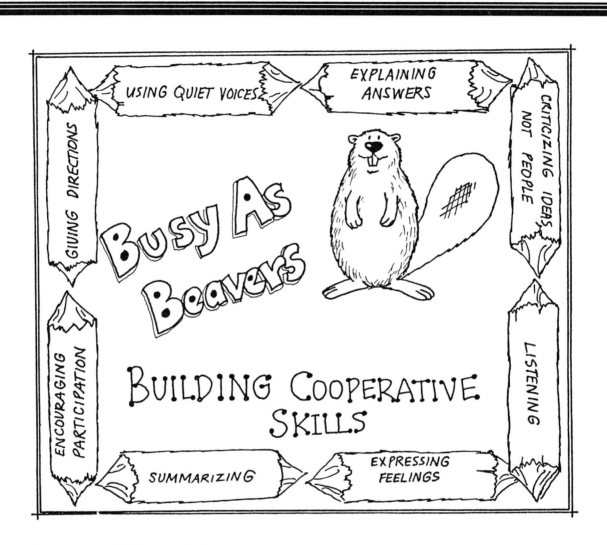

Suggested Materials
- Green paper for background
- Brown paper for beaver, logs, and caption

Construction
Cover bulletin board with green paper. Draw the beaver on brown paper. (You may enlarge illustration and use as pattern, or project onto brown paper.) Outline and mark the features of the beaver using a black marker. Place the figure on the right side of the bulletin board. Place the caption "Busy As Beavers Building Cooperative Skills" on the left side of the board.

Border
Make enlarged copies of the log in illustration. Using a black marker, write cooperative skills on the logs and place them around the border.

Building A Foundation For Cooperative Skills

USING QUIET VOICES

Instruction Phase
Construct the bulletin board shown above.

Suggested Materials
- Red background
- Black caption

Construction
Cover the bulletin board with red paper. Project and trace the big mouth boy onto white paper. Outline him in black. Color "Big Mouth" on his shirt red. Place the figure in the center of the board. Above the figure, place the caption "Don't be a Big Mouth." Under the figure, place the caption "Use Quiet Voices."

BUILDING A FOUNDATION FOR COOPERATIVE SKILLS

Border
A standard border may be purchased from a local school supply store OR you may make a border with many synonyms for quiet and noisy (a pattern is provided on page 27).

Student Understanding Phase
Have students demonstrate what they perceive to be the appropriate level of conversation during a group activity. Then ask the class to judge which student was able to best demonstrate the most suitable voice.

On the chalkboard write the following open-ended statement and lead the class in suggesting phrases that could complete it. (See possible sentence endings below.)

I know I am using a quiet voice when . . .
> . . . only my group members can hear me.
> . . . I am talking slightly above a whisper.
> . . . my voice can't be heard above everyone in my class.
> . . . my teacher tells me I'm using a quiet voice.
> . . . I don't feel as if I'm shouting.

Practice Phase
Using the teacher observation sheet on page 64, inform the class that you are going to be observing each group. You will stand near each group for one minute. If during this one minute observation period all members of the group use quiet voices, then the group will receive a tally mark on the sheet. At the end of the class period, the group with the most tallies will receive a reward. (Observation hint: While watching the groups, bring attention to the groups that are doing a good job.)

Processing Phase
Discuss the observation sheet with the class. Allow students to comment on what the classroom environment was like during the activity. Finish the lesson by writing the following open-ended sentence on the board. Ask students to complete it. (Suggestions are listed below.)

Using quiet voices is a good idea because . . .
> . . . the class is quieter.
> . . . everyone can hear the other group members.
> . . . I can think better.
> . . . the class doesn't get too loud.
> . . . the other groups don't hear your answers.

Maintenance Phase
Continue to observe the "quiet voices" skill, using the teacher's observation sheet. Occasionally you may give every class member three tokens before a cooperative activity begins. Instruct the class that if you hear that someone is not using a quiet voice, that student must give you one token. At the conclusion of the activity, the group with the most tokens left will receive a reward.

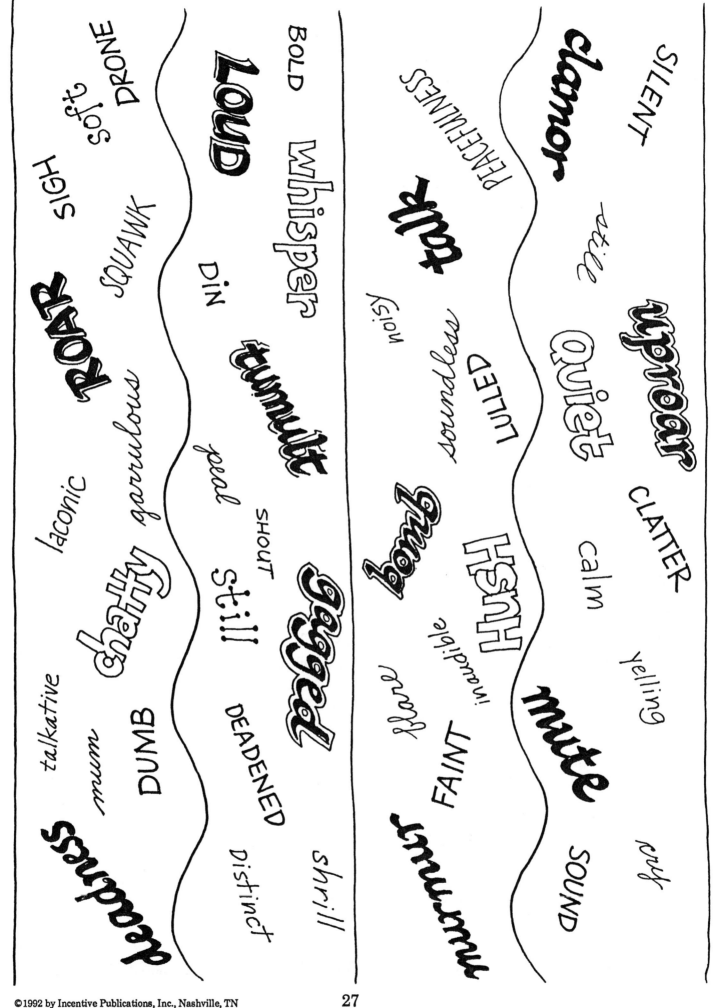

BUILDING A FOUNDATION FOR COOPERATIVE SKILLS

ENCOURAGING PARTICIPATION

Instruction Phase
Write the following definition on the blackboard:

> **Participation:** taking part with others in an activity.

Relate this vignette to the class:
Edwin and Bill are computer partners in the classroom. They are allowed only fifteen minutes of computer time to share, and Bill uses up most of the time. He turns on the computer, puts in the disk, boots it up, grabs the joystick, and plays the game. He simply ignores Edwin when Edwin asks him for a turn with the computer. When the teacher tells Bill to share, he gives Edwin the joystick for a minute or two, then he grabs it back. Edwin might as well just stay at his desk. It's a miserable situation.

Student Understanding Phase
Begin by asking the class to address the following questions:

1. What exactly is the problem?
2. What can the teacher do to solve this problem?
3. Can Edwin solve the problem without the teacher's help?
4. How do you think Bill feels toward Edwin?
5. Can you think of a situation in which you felt like Edwin?

Ask the class to try to devise a cooperative plan to solve this problem. Emphasize that both boys should be permitted to participate equally in the computer time.

Practice Phase
Place each student in a cooperative group made of four students. Give each group an assignment that must be completed by writing answers on paper. The first problem or question is read by a student in the group. She then passes the answer sheet to the student on the right. That student must write the answer. If the student does not know the answer, the group can help—but it is the second student who must write the answer on the answer sheet. When the first question is answered, the sheet is again passed to the

BUILDING A FOUNDATION FOR COOPERATIVE SKILLS

right. The third student reads the question and passes the sheet to the fourth student. The fourth student writes the answer down for the second question. This procedure continues until the worksheet is completed.

Processing Phase

At the close of the activity, ask the groups to turn their worksheets face down. Student 1 numbers from 1 to 4 on the back of the sheet and passes the sheet to Student 2. Student 2 answers Question 1 and passes the sheet to Student 3. Student 3 answers Question 2 and passes the sheet to Student 4, who answers Question 3 and passes the sheet to Student 1. Student 1 answers Question 4.

Question 1: Did everyone in the group participate equally?

Question 2: Why is it important that everyone participate?

Question 3: What was the best thing the group did today?

Question 4: What can the group do next time to ensure equal participation?

The worksheet may be handed to the teacher for assessment, or a class discussion may be conducted.

Maintenance Phase

Suggestion 1:

Give each member of the group only a part of the materials that are necessary to complete the assignment. For example, each member of a five-person group could be given 10 pieces of a 50-piece puzzle. The puzzle will be completed by the group, with student placing the 10 pieces he or she was given.

Suggestion 2:

A "magic microphone" (Hill and Hill, 1990) can be used with young children to help them learn to take turns when speaking. Decorate a paper towel roll so that is resembles a microphone. The microphone will be passed around a group of students. Only the child holding the microphone may speak.

Suggestion 3:

Assign each group member an equal number of chips or strips of paper. Whenever a member of the team contributes an idea, he or she places a chip in the center of the table. When a student runs out of chips, he or she may not contribute again until everyone is out of chips. Then the chips are redistributed, and the members start over again.

BUILDING A FOUNDATION FOR COOPERATIVE SKILLS

EXPLAINING ANSWERS

Yeah, but can you explain it ?

Instruction Phase
Construct this bulletin board.

Suggested Materials
• Yellow background paper
• Posterboard
• Colored markers
• Black Construction Paper

Construction
Enlarge "Einstein and his friend" and trace them onto white posterboard (or project directly onto posterboard). Allow the students to color the figures. Place the figures on a yellow-paper-covered bulletin board and place the caption (in black letters) near the friend of Einstein.

Student Understanding Phase
Using the bulletin board as a focal point, ask the students why it is important not only to be able to do a skill, but also to be able to explain it to others. You might put the equation "2 x 3 = 6" on the board and ask one student to explain why it is true. All the students could then offer other problems, questions, or ideas for another student to explain.

Suggestions:
1. Why doesn't the sun burn us up?
2. What makes a word an adjective?
3. Why does Easter come on different days each year?
4. How do you know if a year is a leap year?

BUILDING A FOUNDATION FOR COOPERATIVE SKILLS

Practice Phase
Materials Needed:
- copies of EGGcellent Activity Sheets (pages 32 and 33) for each group
- 4–6 eggs for each group (hard-boiled, if raw eggs would make you nervous)
- A scale for weighing the eggs
- Tape measures
- Thread
- Crayons

Key Question
As a group, how can you decide how to classify the eggs into the categories of Jumbo, Large, and Medium?

Cooperative Skill
Each member of the group must be able to explain the method used to classify the eggs.

Background Information
Egg packaging plants have a rocker arm with a weight on it. If the egg is heavy enough, it tips the arm, passes onto a conveyor belt, and is then packaged. If it is not heavy enough to tip the arm, it automatically moves to another rocker arm that has a lighter weight. If an egg weighs less than 1.5 ounces it does not go to the stores. A carton of jumbo eggs must weigh 30 ounces, so each jumbo egg must weigh 2.5 ounces. Large eggs weigh 2 ounces each, and medium eggs weigh 1.75 ounces. (From *How Do They Do That?* by Caroline Sutton.)

Student Activity
Permit students to work in groups and complete the "EGGcellent Activity Sheet." When all groups have finished, select at random one egg and one student from each cooperative group. Ask the student to come forward and explain how the egg was classified.

Processing Phase
Have the students answer the following questions:
1. Did you clearly understand how your group classified the eggs?
2. Did you want to explain the method to the class?
3. Did the members of the group help each other prepare for explaining the classification to the class?
4. What was the best thing your group did cooperatively?

Maintenance Phase
Continue class demonstrations throughout the year in order to maintain the skill of explaining answers.

EGGcellent Activity

Names _____

_____

A. ROLES
Decide cooperatively which students will have the following roles:

Runner – The student who can raise his or her hand to ask a question of the teacher.

_____
(Place name here)

Recorder – The student who will fill out this worksheet.

_____
(Place name here)

Checker – The student that makes sure everyone can *explain the activity*. The checker will double-check this worksheet, too.

_____
(Place name here)

Egghandler – This student ensures the safety of the eggs.

_____
(Place name here)

B. PROCEDURE
- Secure 6 eggs for the group. (Remember, Egghandler, we're counting on you.)
- Using the scale, tape measure, or thread, cooperatively measure each egg.
- Working together, devise a method to classify the egg into 3 categories, Jumbo, Large, and Medium.
- Later, one group member will have to explain the group's classification method, so be certain that every group member can classify eggs!
- Place the eggs where everyone can see them.
- Discuss how they could be classified. Think about how they look, what they weigh, and what they measure.

C. WORKSHEET

1. Using a crayon, label the eggs A, B, C, D, E, and F

2. On the lines below, write the classification instructions.

   A **Jumbo** egg is one that _____

   _____ .

   A **Large** egg is one that _____

   _____ .

   A **Medium** egg is one that _____

   _____ .

3. Fill in the chart below.

Egg	(Jumbo, Large, Medium) Type of Egg	Explanation of its classification
A.		
B.		
C.		
D.		
E.		
F.		

4. Make certain each member can explain how your group classified eggs. One of you will be called on to explain it to the class. (Checker—get busy.)

BUILDING A FOUNDATION FOR COOPERATIVE SKILLS

CRITICIZING IDEAS, NOT PEOPLE

Instruction Phase
Using the poster on page 35, discuss the motto "Do Not Criticize People." Explain to the class that when criticism is called for, it is important to remember that it is only the person's ideas that should be criticized. Criticizing the person himself is hurtful.

Student Understanding Phase
Using the poster, discuss how someone could tell that this girl is probably criticizing someone. Point out that constructive criticism would probably not look like the girl in the poster. Assist the students in completing a T-Chart like the sample below.

Constructive Criticism

Looks Like	Sounds Like
Pointing to a particular answer on a work sheet	Question #4 is not clear to me.
Looking to find the answer in the text	In the book it says something different.

Practice Phase
Reproduce and cut out the statement cards on pages 36 and 37 and give one to each student. Assign each student a cooperative partner. Show the groups how the statement is criticizing a person instead of an idea. Have students work together to write down two ways to constructively make each remark without criticizing a person.

Processing Phase
Have each group share the constructive statements with the class.

Maintenance Phase
During the next cooperative activity, appoint a student observer (see page 65 for form) to observe the class and report to the class the positive criticisms she observed.

No, stupid! That's not right.	*You don't know anything.*
You are going to make us get an "F."	*Dummy, you are wrong.*
You don't know how to do anything!	*Don't listen to his crazy idea.*
You never get it right.	*You always mess up.*

Wise up, Stupid.	*Shut Up.*
He's clueless.	*Give me the worksheet before you mess up.*
You are making a big mess.	*How stupid can you get?*
You are wrong again.	*He can't even spell "CAT."*

BUILDING A FOUNDATION FOR COOPERATIVE SKILLS

SUMMARIZING

Instruction Phase

The teacher should read "The Three Little Pigs" to the class. After this familiar story is read, the teacher should instruct the students to answer the following questions:

1. **Who** is in the story?
2. **What** is the problem?
3. **When** did the story take place?
4. **Where** did it take place?
5. **Why** did it happen?

Explain that answering these five questions (or similar questions that begin with **Who, What, When, Where,** or **Why**) is a simple way to summarize information.

Student Understanding

As a class, discuss the answers to the five questions listed above. Discover who in the class is able to be the most concise with the answers.

Practice Phase

Divide the class into cooperative groups. Assign each group a simple nursery rhyme to summarize by creating a newspaper headline for each rhyme. Group roles could include:

1. **Reader:** This student reads the rhyme aloud for the group.
2. **Recorder:** This student is responsible for writing down the newspaper headline for the rhyme.
3. **Questioner:** This student asks the group the **Who, What, When, Where,** and **How** questions. (There may not be an answer for every one of the questions.)
4. **Presenter:** This student reads the headline to the class.

Suggested rhymes are given on page 39. Instruct the class that each rhyme must be summarized by making it into an exciting headline.

Processing Phase

The reader and the presenter from each group are called upon to read the original rhyme and the headline. Through class discussion, students decide if each headline is adequate.

Maintenance Phase

After any cooperative group activity, each group may write a short summary of the cooperative work that was accomplished.

BUILDING A FOUNDATION FOR COOPERATIVE SKILLS

SUGGESTED RHYMES

Three Blind Mice

Three blind mice! Three blind mice! See how they run! See how they run!
They all ran after the farmer's wife,
Who cut off their tails with a carving knife.
Did you ever see such a sight in your life
As three blind mice?

Little Jack Horner

Little Jack Horner
Sat in the Corner,
Eating a Christmas pie;
He put in his thumb,
And pulled out a plum,
And said, "What a good boy am I!"

The Crooked Sixpence

There was a crooked man, and he went a crooked mile,
He found a crooked sixpence beside a crooked stile;
He bought a crooked cat, which caught a crooked mouse,
And they all lived together in a little crooked house.

There Was An Old Woman

There was an old woman who lived in a shoe.
She had so many children she didn't know what to do.
She gave them some broth without any bread.
She whipped them all soundly and put them to bed.

Ding, Dong, Bell

Ding, dong, bell,
Pussy's in the well!
Who put her in?
Little Tommy Lin.
Who pulled her out?
Little Johnny Stout.
What a naughty boy was that,
To try to drown poor pussy-cat,
Who never did him any harm,
But killed the mice in his father's barn.

BUILDING A FOUNDATION FOR COOPERATIVE SKILLS

ENCOURAGING

Instruction Phase
Construct the bulletin board shown above.

Suggested Materials
- Blue background paper
- Posterboard
- Colored markers
- Fabric (optional)
- Yarn (optional)

Construction
Cover the bulletin board with the blue background paper. Project the student figures onto posterboard and trace, or enlarge by some other means. Cut out figures and color them to reflect the ethnic and racial make-up of the students in the class. Yarn and fabric may also be added to the figures to give a three-dimensional effect to the bulletin board. Add the title "Encouraging Words Heard Here." In the caption bubbles, write encouraging remarks. Suggestions:
- Now I understand.
- Thanks for explaining that.
- That's a great idea.
- You are doing a great job.
- That really helped me.

Staple the figures and the caption to the bulletin board.

BUILDING A FOUNDATION FOR COOPERATIVE SKILLS

Border
Standard border may be purchased from the local school supply store, or ask students to trace around their hands. Each should cut out his hand pattern and write an encouraging remark on the hand. Place the hands around the edges of the board.

Student Understanding
On a large sheet of lined chart tablet paper, write the following statements:

1. What a dumb idea.
2. Thanks for helping me.
3. You are good at fractions.
4. Gross, that's a terrible answer.
5. You do excellent work.
6. That's messy.
7. I wish you weren't in this group.
8. Everybody is helping.
9. We finished quickly.
10. That's a great answer.

Have the class write down which of the ten responses were encouraging (2, 3, 5, 8, 9, and 10). Then ask the students to write five encouraging remarks and five discouraging remarks. Share the responses with the class.

Practice Phase
Assign a cooperative activity. Using the Teacher Observation Form on page 64, observe each group. Stand next to each group for two minutes. Place a tally on the sheet for each encouraging remark that is heard. Then move to another group and listen for encouraging remarks.

Processing Phase
Discuss the observation form with the entire class. Attempt to recall specific encouraging remarks made by class members. Reward the group that had the most encouraging remarks.

Maintenance Phase
Continue teacher observation during other activities. Be certain to verbally praise students who are encouraging others.

BUILDING A FOUNDATION FOR COOPERATIVE SKILLS

LISTENING

Introduction Phase
Read the following vignette to the class:

I can't stand to talk to Terry. I tell a great story, and he looks at everybody except me. He asks me a question that I answered just a minute ago. He sometimes interrupts me right in the middle of a sentence. To top it off, he will later say that I didn't tell him the story. What is his problem?

Ask the class to define Terry's problem. (He's not listening.)

Student Understanding Phase
On the board, write the following open-ended sentence:

I can tell someone is listening when . . .

Possible student responses:
   ... she is looking me in the eye.
   ... he nods his head.
   ... she smiles.
   ... he does not interrupt.
   ... she asks me a question that is about my story.

Practice Phase
Organize the students into cooperative groups, each made up of two students. Give each group a penny. Assign a section of a textbook or newspaper to read. One student tosses the penny, and the other student "calls it" in the air. If the student calls heads and the penny lands on heads, he gets to read a paragraph to the other student. If he calls heads and the penny lands on tails, he is the listener. The student who tossed the coin is the reader. The listener then tells the reader what she heard. Together they decide what the paragraph meant. Then they "re-toss" the coin and the process begins again. Remember, "Heads you read, tails you listen."

Processing
Complete the LISTEN UP processing sheet on page 43. The teacher may choose to collect the LISTEN UP processing sheet, or the class members may discuss their responses.

Maintenance
After another cooperative activity, have the class complete a T-Chart on Listening.

LISTEN UP PROCESSING SHEET

Name _____

Directions: During the cooperative activity, you are to be an active listener. Place a check by each behavior you demonstrated.

While I was practicing listening, I:
_____1. Didn't interrupt the reader.
_____2. Looked at the reader.
_____3. Paid close attention to the reader.
_____4. Nodded at the reader.
_____5. Smiled at the reader.
_____6. Restated facts from the reading.
_____7. Asked questions about the reading.

On a scale of 1 to 10 (10 being a great listener) I believe I deserve a _____.

LISTEN UP PROCESSING SHEET

Name _____

Directions: During the cooperative activity, you are to be an active listener. Place a check by each behavior you demonstrated.

While I was practicing listening, I:
_____1. Didn't interrupt the reader.
_____2. Looked at the reader.
_____3. Paid close attention to the reader.
_____4. Nodded at the reader.
_____5. Smiled at the reader.
_____6. Restated facts from the reading.
_____7. Asked questions about the reading.

On a scale of 1 to 10 (10 being a great listener) I believe I deserve a _____.

BUILDING A FOUNDATION FOR COOPERATIVE SKILLS

EXPRESSING FEELINGS

Instruction Phase
Using the poster on page 45, discuss the motto "When life gives you lemons, make lemonade!" What does this motto mean? When have you made lemonade from a lemon in your own life?

Student Understanding
Allow the students to make "emotion buttons." If a button-maker is available, that's great! If one is not available, simply cut out circles that have diameters of at least 2½ inches. The students write a slogan or a feeling on the button. Have plenty of bright markers for the students to use. When completed, the students may pin the buttons on their clothing.

Practice Phase
Reproduce the EXPRESSING FEELINGS Activity Page (page 46) and have each student complete a copy.

Processing Phase
Have a group discussion of the responses on the EXPRESSING FEELINGS Activity Page.

Maintenance Phase
Have students complete the group processing sheet on page 47.

When life gives you lemons

make lemonade

EXPRESSING FEELINGS—<u>PRACTICE</u>

Name_____

Read the following situation descriptions. Put yourself in the main character's place. What would you think? How would you feel? What action would you take?

Situation #1
Susie is in your new cooperative group. She is very quiet. If she speaks, it is only a whisper. The other people in the group are beginning to ignore her.

What do you think about Susie? _____

_____

How would you feel if you were Susie? _____

_____

What action could you take to help Susie? _____

_____

Situation #2
James is such a pain. He acts angry all the time. He makes fun of everybody in the group. He won't do his share of the work. Now everybody else in the group is beginning to argue all the time.

What do you think about James? _____

_____

How would you feel if you were James? _____

_____

What action could you take to help James? _____

_____

Situation #3
Sean thinks he is so smart. He calls everybody "stupid." He won't listen to anyone. He won't explain his answers. He thinks he is a genius.

What do you think about Sean? _____

_____

How would you feel if you were Sean? _____

_____

What action could you take to help Sean? _____

_____

GROUP PROCESSING—EXPRESSING FEELINGS

Name_____

When we are working in a cooperative group, these are the things that make us feel happy:

Things we do _____

_____

Things we say _____

_____

When we are in a cooperative group, these are the things that make us uncomfortable and unhappy:

Things we do _____

_____

Things we say _____

_____

GROUP PROCESSING—EXPRESSING FEELINGS

Name_____

When we are working in a cooperative group, these are the things that make us feel happy:

Things we do _____

_____

Things we say _____

_____

When we are in a cooperative group, these are the things that make us uncomfortable and unhappy:

Things we do _____

_____

Things we say _____

_____

BUILDING A FOUNDATION FOR COOPERATIVE SKILLS

GIVING DIRECTIONS TO THE GROUP

Instruction Phase

Ask each student to draw on a plain sheet of paper the design pictured below, but do not show the students the design. *Describe* the design verbally, attempting to give clear directions. If possible, give rulers to the students.

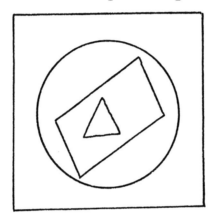

Student Understanding Phase

After students complete their drawings, select a few students to share their work with the class. Then reveal the original drawing. By comparing and contrasting the students' interpretations, the class can discuss which of the teacher's directions were most helpful.

Practice Phase

Each student is to complete the worksheet on page 49. Working in cooperative groups of two, each student will attempt to sketch the drawing that her partner describes.

Processing Phase

Have each cooperative group mount its sketches and descriptions onto a large sheet of construction paper. Permit the students to discuss methods of clarifying instructions.

Maintenance Phase

Periodically assign the role of "direction giver" to a member of a cooperative group. One method of doing this is to permit one student from each group to receive directions directly from the teacher. That student returns to his group and gives the instructions. This works particularly well for art and crafts projects, games, or for introducing new computer software.

GIVING DIRECTIONS

Name_____

Without showing ANYONE, sketch a simple design below. Then write a description of the design on the lines below. Be clear and concise. After you and your cooperative group finish these first two steps, one of you will read your description while the other attempts to draw the design. No questions can be asked! No pointing! After you finish, switch roles and try to draw your partner's design from his or her description.

STEP 1:   **STEP 2:**

Sketch Design	Written Description

BUILDING A FOUNDATION FOR COOPERATIVE SKILLS

ASKING PROBING QUESTIONS

Instruction Phase
Instruct the class to pretend that a new boy is enrolling in school today. The students' job is to find out as much about him as possible. The challenge is that the entire class cannot ask any more than five questions. Have the class suggest ten questions to ask the new student. Working as a class, narrow the ten questions down to just five.

Student Understanding Phase
Discuss with the class the following question. "Why is it important to know how to ask good, probing questions?" Suggestions to aid in the discussion:
– There are problems that need solutions.   – You need more information.
– You need to make important decisions.   – You need to organize your thoughts.
– There are many things you don't understand. – You are curious.

Practice Phase
Place the students in groups of four. Each group is to play **20 Questions.** One student in the group picks a historical figure. The other three members of the group have the opportunity to ask 20 **yes** or **no** questions. The group should try to discover which historical figure the first group member selected. Suggestions: Neil Armstrong, George Washington, Noah, President George Bush, Santa Claus.
If the first group member selected John Kennedy, possible questions could be:

Is it a he?	Was it George Washington?	Was he President in the 60's?
Is/was he a President?	Was it Abe Lincoln?	Was he shot?
Is he living?	Was he President in the 70's?	Was he John Kennedy?

Processing Phase
Each cooperative group selects a historical figure. Then a member of one group comes to the front of the room and the class tries to guess who the person is, using 20 or fewer questions. The class attempts to discover who the group selected. During this time, the teacher will make comments on the students' ability to ask good questions.

Maintenance Phase
Before beginning another cooperative activity, appoint a student observer for each group (see Student Observation Form, page 65). The student observers should be instructed to look for the skill of "asking probing questions." The observer does not speak to the group. She is there only to observe. Each time she believes that a group member has asked a good question, she puts a tally by the student's name. After the cooperative activity is done, the observer can show the form to her group and discuss the results.

QUICK IDEAS TO MAKE
COOPERATIVE LEARNING EASIER

ORGANIZING TEAMS

Formally Organizing Teams

One of the things that differentiates Cooperative Learning from group work is the way the groups are organized. In Cooperative Learning, the teacher organizes each group so that it contains one high-achieving student, two average-achieving students, and one low-achieving student. The groups should also be balanced racially and sexually. For more detailed information about how to organize groups in this way, refer to pages 10-14 in *The Middle Grades Teacher's Handbook For Cooperative Learning* (Incentive Publications, 1991).

Sometimes a teacher needs to organize cooperative groups quickly without taking the time to do so formally. For this reason, a couple of quick ways to organize groups follows.

Numbering Off

Before students begin numbering off, the teacher needs to decide if the number of groups or the number of students in each group is more important. If a teacher has 20 students in a class and knows that a particular activity needs exactly four students, then the teacher needs five groups of four students. With this in mind, ask the students to number off from one to five. All of the "ones" will form a group, all of the "twos" will form a group, and so on. However, sometimes a teacher knows he has enough materials for exactly six groups, and it is more important to have six groups than it is to have exactly four in a group. In this case, ask the class to number off from one to six even though the groups may not all be the same size.

Birthday Count-Off

This is very similar to numbering off except the students must first put themselves in order according to birthday. To make this more challenging and to emphasize cooperation, ask the students to do this without talking. Once the students are in birthday order, number off to form groups.

Playing Cards

Another quick way to organize cooperative groups involves randomly handing out playing cards. If the class has 28 students, hand out the "aces" through the "sevens." After the cards are shuffled, hand out the cards as the students walk in the door, or walk around the room and ask each student to draw a card. All of the "aces" form a group, all of the "twos" form a group, and so on. One advantage of using this method is that it allows roles to be assigned quickly. Simply tell the students that all students holding hearts will be runners today, all spades will be checkers, all clubs will be encouragers, and all diamonds will be recorders.

The Co-Leader Approach

For this particular method, the teacher identifies the higher-achieving students, the middle-achieving students, and the lower-achieving students. The teacher will pair one high-achieving student with one low-achieving student. The students should not be told they are high- or low-achieving.

Now the rest of the class will be in the middle achievement range. Allow each pair of students to choose one of the remaining students to join their team. Remind the class that the groups should be mixed racially and sexually.

After each pair has chosen one other member, the new three-person group may again choose someone from the remaining students to join the group. Continue until all students have been placed in a cooperative group.

These groups will be naturally balanced by achievement since the teacher placed high and low students together and all remaining students are middle-achieving. Care should be taken to ensure that the groups do not end up all boy or all girl. This way of grouping does give students an opportunity to have a limited voice in the determination of their teams. Choosing friends should not be prohibited.

Pair Ups

The teacher will divide the students into four groups, HIGH, HIGH/MIDDLE, LOW/MIDDLE, and LOW, without explaining to the students why or how they were placed in particular groups. Then, HIGH students will choose LOW students to form a pair. HIGH/MIDDLE students will choose LOW/MIDDLE students to form a pair. At this point the HIGH LOW pairs are on one side of the classroom and the HIGH/MIDDLE LOW/MIDDLE pairs are on the other side of the classroom. Each pair must now join with another pair on the opposite side of the classroom. (Adapted from Pairs Pair in Spencer Kagan's book *Cooperative Learning Resources for Teachers.*)

QUICK IDEAS TO MAKE COOPERATIVE LEARNING EASIER

IDENTIFYING STUDENT ROLES

Now that your students have been organized into cooperative groups, it would be helpful to identify publicly the role of each member of the team. One way to identify roles is to write the names of the team members on the team chart, using a different color for each role. For example, the Runner could be written in red, the Recorder in blue, the Checker in green, and the Encourager in orange. To help students know which role each color identifies, put the posters explaining each role on the bulletin board and underline the title of each role in the appropriate color. Or you may wish to reproduce role posters (pages 85-88) on paper in the appropriate colors.

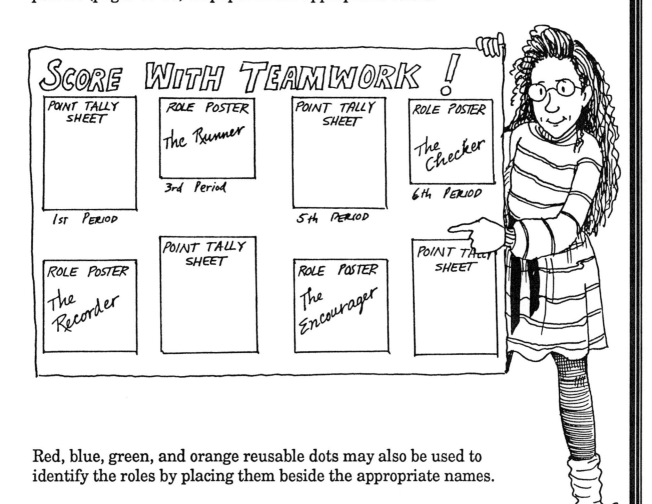

Red, blue, green, and orange reusable dots may also be used to identify the roles by placing them beside the appropriate names.

Another way to identify the students' roles is to place a colored removable dot on each student's desk. This way each team member, and the teacher, can identify at a glance a person's role.

QUICK IDEAS TO MAKE COOPERATIVE LEARNING EASIER

ORGANIZING DESKS

One quick and effective way to organize the class seating chart in cooperative groups is to use 1½" by 2" self-sticking note pads. Student name, team assignment, and student role can be written on each note sheet. Then, using a large sheet of paper, the note sheets can be placed in group seatings. Be sure to label the teacher's desk and any other distinguishing features. This will help students know where their desks are to be arranged during cooperative activities. If possible, the teacher may want to make a copy of the chart for each student in the class. Posting the original chart on a bulletin board for the students may be helpful. If the chart is to be used in this way, reproduce it and laminate it first.

TEACHER

QUICK IDEAS TO MAKE COOPERATIVE LEARNING EASIER

Sometimes teachers would like to do a cooperative activity without having to spend a lot of time organizing a formal seating chart. One possible solution is to use masking tape to mark X's or numbers on the floor of the classroom. When it is time to break up into groups, simply ask each team to move to one of the areas. This way the students will be spread out over the classroom instead of sitting too close together.

Some activities are more easily accomplished if tables are used rather than desks. Since most schools are equipped with a science lab that has tables and chairs, explore the possibility of using the science lab. If a teacher is permanently assigned to the lab, swapping classrooms for the day may be an option. If your school doesn't have a science lab, or if you are unable to use it, check into using the tables in the cafeteria. And, of course, there are usually tables in the school library.

Another classroom management strategy is to mark the table that is to be used by a team before the students arrive. This will keep chaos to a minimum. If teams have names, label each table with their name. If teams do not have names, color code or label each table with numbers.

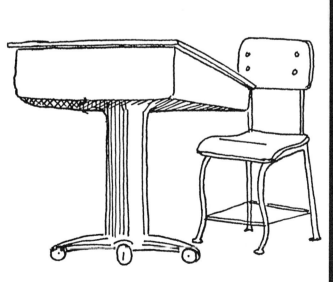

In Spencer Kagan's book, *Cooperative Learning Resources for Teachers*, Manuel Robles suggests using string to hang coat hangers above each team's work space. Each team would be responsible for making a paper team name sign that could be folded to hang over the bottom wire of the coat hanger. This would be very useful in classrooms that are departmentalized because the signs could easily be changed each class period and it would not matter if the signs hung over tables, or over the places where the teacher wants each team to move their desks.

QUICK IDEAS TO MAKE COOPERATIVE LEARNING EASIER

SIMPLE WAYS TO INCORPORATE COOPERATIVE LEARNING INTO THE CLASSROOM ROUTINE

The following are simple methods for introducing Cooperative Learning into the regular learning environment.

We'll Do The Even, And Then You'll Do The Odd

Allow the students to work in cooperative groups to complete the even-numbered exercises in the textbook. The group is to give the teacher a consensus paper.

Then the students will return to their own seats and complete the odd exercises in the textbook. Each student must turn in a paper with the completed odd problems. An individual grade is given on this assignment.

Two By Two Drill

Divide a cooperative group of four into two groups of two students each. Each student quizzes his partner on the selected material. Then the pairs swap partners and continue the review.

Homework Checkup!

After students come to class with their homework completed, permit the cooperative groups to meet and discuss the assignment. The group must agree on a set of answers for the assignment. The group's consensus paper is graded. If the assignment had a great deal of writing, the teacher may want to give each group a pair of scissors, a large sheet of unlined paper, and rubber cement. The group quickly cuts out correct answers from different group member's papers and glues them onto unlined paper.

QUICK IDEAS TO MAKE COOPERATIVE LEARNING EASIER

Testing Tune-Up

The day before an individual test is to be given, allow the cooperative groups to meet and take a practice test. Many textbooks have a chapter review worksheet that could be easily used for this activity. Instruct the cooperative groups to complete the practice test cooperatively during the class period. When the practice test is completed, instruct each cooperative group to exchange papers with another cooperative group. Reward the group that had the best score. If time permits, allow the groups to reassemble and correct any errors. During the next class period, the individual students will take the actual test.

Group Interdependent Study Activity

If the teacher has found that the students are still too dependent on the teacher rather than on each other, a group interdependent study activity is in order. Assign a task to the group, and state that the group must complete the assignment without the assistance of the teacher. If the group members want the teacher to help, inform them that they must do the activity without help. Suggest that a certain group member may be able to help. Another suggestion is to specifically point out each group member's strengths in the subject. After the group has become involved in the assignment, the teacher may then help the groups.

Cooperative Group Relays

Instruct the cooperative groups to sit in rows. Hand the first person in each row a worksheet. This student writes down the first answer, and then passes the worksheet to the next person in the group. The second student answers the second question, and passes it to the next group member. This format continues until the worksheet is complete. When the cooperative group finishes the entire worksheet, the runner in the group takes the worksheet to the teacher. The teacher checks it quickly. The group reassembles and corrects any errors. The first group to finish with all problems correct wins the relay.

HOW TO USE FORMS

Letters To Parents

When students are beginning to use Cooperative Learning in the classroom, parents need to be notified. Sample letters are given on pages 62 and 63. To use one of these letters, or one of your own, reproduce on the school letterhead and add your signature.

Teacher Observation Form

Use the Teacher Observation Form on page 64 to evaluate the cooperative skill each team is practicing for the day. The teacher chooses one or two cooperative skills for everyone to work on during class time. See page 21 for suggestions. Write the skill(s) to be observed on the chart. As the groups begin their work, move around the classroom, spending about one minute observing each group. As the cooperative skill is used, make a tally mark on the Teacher Observation Form under that skill. At the end of the class, the teacher should meet briefly with each group to discuss what was observed and to help the students make decisions about how to improve their skills.

Student Observation Form

Sometimes a team has trouble with a particular skill and shows no signs of improving. One way to help is to assign a student observer for the day. This student may be the student the teacher believes is having trouble with the particular skill, or a student that the teacher believes will be particularly observant and fair in the evaluation. The Student Observation Form on page 65 will help the observer. The student observer will remove herself from the activity the rest of the group is working on for the day and will mark only the appropriate use of a cooperative skill when she sees it.

At the end of the activity, the student observer will share her findings with the rest of the group and together the group will work to come up with a plan to overcome the problem.

COOPERATIVE LEARNING TEACHING AIDS

Student Self-Assessment Form

It is important for students to evaluate their own growth in cooperative skills. Often a student's self-evaluation does not match the teacher's evaluation. When this occurs, the teacher and student need to discuss how they arrived at their differing opinions. It may be that the teacher does not have the "whole picture," and needs to hear the student's explanation in order to evaluate fairly. The Student Self-Assessment Form on page 66 may be particularly helpful.

Daily Goal Form

As the students begin to assess themselves, it is important for each to develop a plan to overcome his weaknesses. One way to accomplish this is to allow each student to develop daily goals. The teacher could give each student a copy of the form on page 68. The student writes his name on it along with his goal for the day. If the goal for that day is to use a quiet voice, the student would make a tally mark under the "thumbs up" heading every time he caught himself using a quiet voice. Every time he caught himself talking too loudly, he would make a tally mark under the "thumbs down" heading.

Since the students are choosing their goals for the day and are marking their own successes, they are much more likely to make an effort to do well.

Group Processing Inventory

The Group Processing Inventory found on page 69 is very useful in helping the group to pull together to work cooperatively and develop good social interaction skills. It also forces the group members to publicly announce whether they helped every member of the group to understand the assignment. Before each cooperative activity, the teacher should announce the cooperative skill that everyone will be working on for that day. As each group finishes the assignment, its members will fill out the group processing inventory. Review of these inventories helps the teacher to see areas of growth.

COOPERATIVE LEARNING TEACHING AIDS

Cooperative Skills Assessment Form

Just as the teacher needs to evaluate the progress the students are making in academics, the teacher will also need to evaluate progress and development of cooperative skills. One way to do this is to use a Cooperative Skills Assessment Form. This form can be found on page 67.

Point Tally Sheet

The Point Tally Sheet (page 71) is a useful way to keep up with the points each member of a team has earned on her individual work. Before discussing how to use the Point Tally Sheet in the classroom, a review of the point system is necessary.

The point system is effective for two major reasons. First, it is a wonderful way to pull every member of a team together to work toward a common goal. That goal is to accumulate more points than any other team in order to earn a reward. Second, students are competing only with themselves when they earn points. Since some students may never be able to earn "A"s, but may be able to improve their base scores enough to earn 3 team points, the point system is an outstanding way to boost the self-esteem of some lower-achieving students. These students become valuable to the team as they continue to show improvement and to earn points. The higher-achieving members will be more than willing to spend additional time helping the lower-achieving students to fully understand the material when they see they have a stake in the kind of grades every member of the team makes.

Before students were assigned to cooperative groups, the teacher should have determined a base score. This score may have been the last six weeks' grade on the report card, the final grade on the report card from the previous year, or it may have been the grade a student made on a pretest of the upcoming material. This base score is useful in assigning students to teams. It is also used to determine how much a student is improving so that team points may be assigned. Students usually have the opportunity to earn team points when they are working on individual papers or taking

COOPERATIVE LEARNING
TEACHING AIDS

a test over material they have practiced with teammates. Students earn points for their team based on this chart:

Test Score or Individual Paper	Points Earned for Group
A Perfect Score	3
10 or more points above base score	3
5 to 9 points above base score	2
4 points above to 4 points below base score	1
5 or more points below base score	0

The Point Tally Sheet may be used by the teacher only, or it may be used on a bulletin board to publicly display the current team point standings of every team. Students' names need to be written on the Tally Sheet, grouped according to teams. There is a place at the top of the Tally Sheet, under team assignments, to write the name of the assignment that resulted in the team points. If the Tally Sheet will be used only by the teacher, write each student's base score in the first column to make it faster to assign team points. If the Tally Sheet will be displayed on a bulletin board, do not display each student's grade. Instead, place a clear sheet of acetate over the Point Tally Sheet. Write each student's base score next to his name in the appropriate column on the acetate sheet. This way the teacher can quickly place this over the Tally Sheet and easily assign team points. As teams accumulate points, interest in which team has the most points will rise. To help students know at a glance which team is ahead, put a reusable sticker next to the high-scoring team in each class.

The Point Tally Sheet on page 71 has space for 25 students. Since many classrooms have more than 25 students, you may want to make two copies of this sheet and attach one to the bottom of the other.

Lesson Plan Guide

A lesson plan form is included to assist the teacher in cooperative planning (see page 72). A cooperative lesson must always include specific instructions for student roles and methods to foster interdependence and group processing.

61

Dear Parents:

During the course of this school year, I will be using many different teaching methods and strategies to help your child to be the best he or she can possibly be. Some of these methods will be familiar to you, but one method, Cooperative Learning, may not.

Cooperative Learning is a teaching method by means of which students work together in structured groups, helping each other learn, and earning rewards for their efforts. Every grading period I will divide the class into small groups containing two to six mixed-ability members. While it will be my primary responsibility to teach skills to all students, every member of a cooperative group is responsible for making sure that he or she knows the material and that every other member of the group knows the material, too.

Students will not be working in groups every day, only on days when the activities lend themselves to group effort. For example, I may ask students to break up into cooperative groups to practice a new skill, write a report, demonstrate a technique, or study for a test. Students will all receive the same grade on cooperative papers, and students may be awarded bonus points for their cooperative efforts on these days.

On the days when students are working individually, a student will receive only the grade he or she earns. I will also assign team points to each team whose members show improvement on these individual papers. Teams will accumulate these points during the grading period, and the team with the most points at the end of the grading period will receive a reward of some kind.

I am committed to using Cooperative Learning in my classroom for two reasons. First, I believe it truly helps students to do better in their studies. Second, business leaders across the nation have applauded the use of Cooperative Learning because it closely mirrors the kinds of activities your children will be engaged in when they enter the work force. Students need to be exposed to a healthy mix of cooperative, as well as competitive, activities during the course of their formal education in order to succeed in the marketplace.

I want to thank you for *your* cooperation with me this year, and I encourage you to contact me at school if you have any questions about Cooperative Learning.

Sincerely,

Dear Parents:

This school year I will be using Cooperative Learning in my classroom. Cooperative Learning is a teaching method by means of which students work together in structured groups, helping each other learn, and earning rewards for their efforts.

I am committed to using Cooperative Learning in my classroom for two reasons. First, I believe it truly helps students to do better in their studies. Second, business leaders across the nation have applauded the use of Cooperative Learning because it closely mirrors the kinds of activities your children will be engaged in when they enter the work force.

Students will not be working in groups every day, only on days when the activities lend themselves to group effort. For example, I may ask students to break up into cooperative groups to practice a new skill, write a report, demonstrate a technique, or study for a test.

I will also assign team points to each team whose members show improvement on their *individual* papers. Teams will accumulate these points during the grading period, and the team with the most points will receive a reward.

I want to thank you for *your* cooperation with me this year, and I encourage you to contact me at school if you have any questions about Cooperative Learning.

Sincerely,

TEACHER OBSERVATION FORM

Observation Date _____

INSTRUCTIONS:

- Select one or two cooperative skills for observation.
- Write down the skills you will observe on the chart below. Stand by each group for one minute; then move to the next group and observe.
- Record each use of the skill with a tally mark in the box under the skill.
- Under comments, note any outstanding displays of the pinpointed skill(s). Later, share the comments with individual groups.

Team Number	Cooperative Skill #1	Cooperative Skill #2	Comments
Team 1			
Team 2			
Team 3			
Team 4			
Team 5			
Team 6			

TEACHER FORM

STUDENT OBSERVATION FORM

Observation Date _____

INSTRUCTIONS:

From the list below, choose one cooperative skill for observation.

- listening
- using quiet voices
- summarizing
- explaining answers
- contributing ideas
- staying on task

Write selected cooperative skill in second column below. Mark tallies in this column every time a student uses this skill.

In the comments column, record any outstanding examples of the use of this skill by a teammate.

Names of Teammates	Cooperative Skill	Comments
1.		
2.		
3.		
4.		
5.		
6.		

STUDENT FORM

STUDENT SELF-ASSESSMENT FORM

STUDENT NAME _____

SKILL	EFFORT	ACHIEVEMENT
Used quiet voice		
Encouraged participation		
Explained answers		
Criticized ideas, not people		
Summarized		
Expressed support		
Listened		
Expressed feeling		
Gave directions		
Asked questions		

KEY: + GOOD   – NEEDS WORK

STUDENT FORM

COOPERATIVE SKILLS ASSESSMENT FORM

STUDENT NAME _____

SKILL	Uses Effectively	Needs Practice
Uses quiet voice		
Encourages participation		
Explains answers		
Criticizes ideas only		
Summarizes		
Expresses support		
Listens		
Expresses feeling		
Gives directions		
Asks questions		

TEACHER FORM

NAME _____ DATE _____

Goal for the Day _____

Place a tally mark here
every time you use the skill.

Place a tally mark here
every time you forget to use
the skill.

NAME _____ DATE _____

Goal for the Day _____

Place a tally mark here
every time you use the skill.

Place a tally mark here
every time you forget to use
the skill.

GROUP PROCESSING INVENTORY

NAME	MY JOB WAS . . .

_____

_____

_____

_____

_____

_____

_____

Circle **Yes** or **No** for the first three statements, and complete statements 4 and 5. The entire group must agree on the selected answers.

1. Everyone in our group helped with the assignment.   **Yes**   **No**

2. We made certain everyone understood the assignment.   **Yes**   **No**

3. We did a good job listening to each other's ideas.   **Yes**   **No**

4. Today the best cooperative thing we did was _____

_____

_____

_____

5. Next time we need to improve by _____

_____

_____

_____

STUDENT FORM

Cooperative Pledge

We agree to work together on this assignment. Everyone in the group must understand all the answers before we write them down. Each member will receive the same grade at the end of the project.

Signed By:

_____   _____

_____   _____

_____   _____

_____   _____

Date:_____

Cooperative Pledge

We agree to work together on this assignment. Everyone in the group must understand all the answers before we write them down. Each member will receive the same grade at the end of the project.

Signed By:

_____   _____

_____   _____

_____   _____

_____   _____

Date:_____

POINT TALLY SHEET

Student Name	Role	Base Score	Individual Assignments									

LESSON PLAN GUIDE FOR COOPERATIVE LEARNING

THE BASICS
These components are found in all lessons.

Subject _____ Grade Level _____

Instructional Objective(s) _____

Materials _____

ORGANIZATION OF COOPERATIVE GROUPS
The organization of the groups depends on class size, materials available, and the types of roles that are needed.

Group Size _____ Roles of Group Members _____

_____

Special Instructions or Organization of Groups _____

_____

LESSON PLAN AND IMPLEMENTATION OF LESSON
Cooperative lessons must incorporate interdependence and accountability.

The Task _____

_____

Positive Interdependence will be fostered by _____

_____

Individual Accountability will be assessed by _____

_____

Group Accountability will be assessed by _____

_____

The Cooperative Skill that will be emphasized _____

CLOSURE—*This is Last, but not Least!*

Group Processing Activity _____

Criteria for Academic Success _____

Reteaching/Reviewing Ideas _____

_____

POSTING
COOPERATIVE LEARNING GROUPS

BULLETIN BOARD IDEA #1

One way to post cooperative groups is to list student names and roles on the Point Tally Sheet, and post the sheet on the bulletin board. This way much of the information needed to keep Cooperative Learning flowing in your classroom is all in one place.

COOPERATIVE GROUPS

POINT TALLY SHEET											
Student Name	**Role**	**Base Score**	**Individual Assignments**								
			~	~	~						
Latonya Jones	Runner		2	3	1						
Larry Smith	Checker		1	2	1						
Phyllis Brown	Recorder	Do not list on bulletin board	3	1	–						
Carlos Sanchez	Encourager		1	2	3						
Hunter Parks	Runner		3	1	1						
Mary Edwards	Checker		2	2	2						
Reginald Meddling	Recorder		1	3	1						
Shante Boyd	Encourager		1	2	3						
Angelica Hernandez	Runner		2	1	–						
Juan Ellis	Checker		3	2	2						
Elizabeth Taylor	Recorder		3	1	1						
Carter Phillips	Encourager		1	3	1						

Suggested Materials
- Background—Newspaper stock market report
- Letters—Red
- Point Tally Sheet reproduced from page 70 (enlarged if possible)

Construction
Cover the bulletin board with the stock market report pages from the newspaper. Laminate the point tally sheet and center it on the board. Above the chart, place the caption "Cooperative Groups."

Border
Use a standard red or black border purchased from a school supply store.

© 1992 by Incentive Publications, Inc., Nashville, TN

BULLETIN BOARD IDEA #2

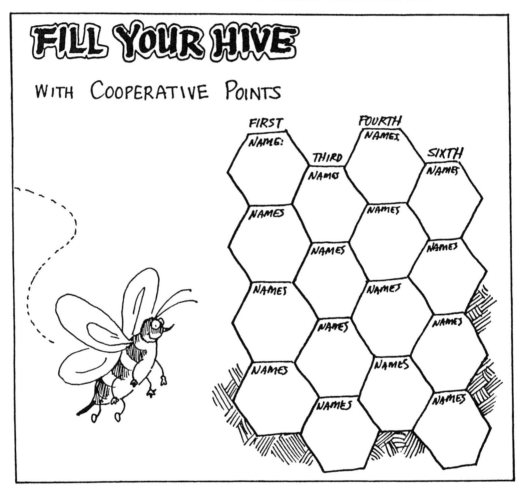

FILL YOUR HIVE

WITH COOPERATIVE POINTS

Suggested Materials
• Yellow background • Black caption

Construction
Cover the bulletin board with yellow paper. Using the hexagon pattern on page 75, reproduce one hexagon for each team. List team names on the lines. (Laminate if possible.) Attach to bulletin board in beehive pattern, as illustrated. Copy, project, or enlarge and trace the bee. Color using yellow and black. Place bee in lower left corner. Place the caption "Fill your hive with cooperative points" across top of the bulletin board. Identify class or subject at the top of each hexagon column.

Border
Use a standard black border purchased from a school supply store.

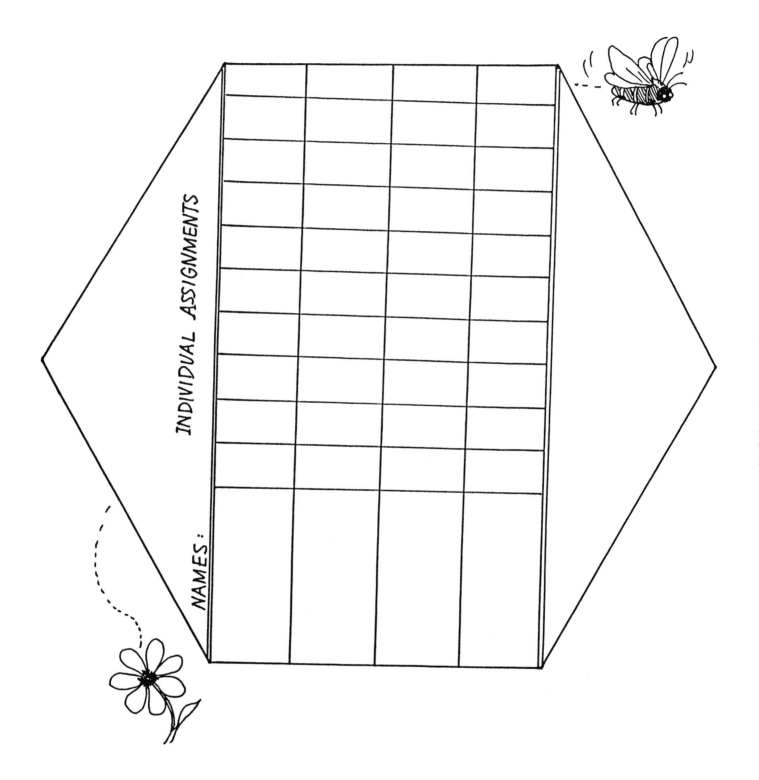

INDIVIDUAL ASSIGNMENTS

NAMES:

75

POSTING
COOPERATIVE LEARNING GROUPS

BULLETIN BOARD IDEA #3

Another way to display your cooperative learning groups is to use the form on page 77 to simply list the group members and their roles.

COOPERATION COUNTS !

FIRST	THIRD	FOURTH	SIXTH
MEMBER / ROLE	MEMBER / ROLE	MEMBER / ROLE	MEMBER / ROLE
MEMBER / ROLE	MEMBER / ROLE	MEMBER / ROLE	MEMBER / ROLE
MEMBER / ROLE	MEMBER / ROLE	MEMBER / ROLE	MEMBER / ROLE
MEMBER / ROLE	MEMBER / ROLE	MEMBER / ROLE	MEMBER / ROLE

Suggested Materials
- Green background
- Yellow caption

Construction
Cover bulletin board with green paper. Reproduce the form from page 77. Write each group's names on a different form. List the groups under the captions "1st Period," "2nd Period," etc. or "Reading," "Math," etc. Center the caption "Cooperation Counts" at the top of the board.

Border
Use a standard yellow border purchased from a school supply store.

MEMBERS	ROLES

MEMBERS	ROLES

BULLETIN BOARD IDEA #4

Suggested Materials
- White background paper
- White posterboard
- Colored markers

Construction
Cover the bulletin board with white background paper. Using an overhead projector, trace the *people* on the white posterboard. Make the *people* as large as the bulletin board will permit. Color the figures with colored markers. Place them in the center of the bulletin board.

Using commercially-made die-cut letters, add the caption "Cooperation is Everybody's Job." List the members of the cooperative groups on large charts and place the group listings around the figure. Reproduce the posters from pages 79 and 80 and color the circles with four different colors. Attach these posters beneath the figures on the bulletin board. Place colored dots next to the names of the students according to the roles they will fill. For example, if you color the circle on the Runner poster red, place red dots beside the names of all Runners on the large charts.

Border
Border may be purchased from a local school supply store, OR a border can be easily made by cutting the classified section of the newspaper into four-inch strips. Place the strips of newspaper around the board.

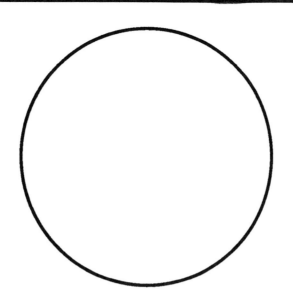

RECORDER–
WRITES DOWN THE ANSWERS

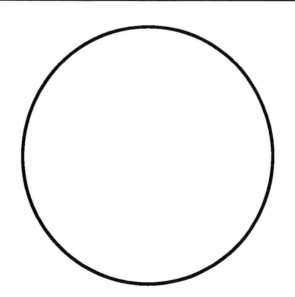

ENCOURAGER–
KEEPS THE GROUP WORKING

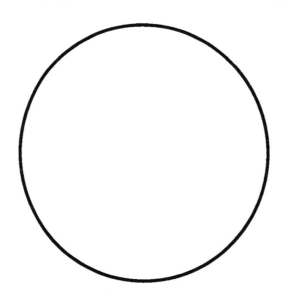

RUNNER–
ASKS THE TEACHER FOR HELP

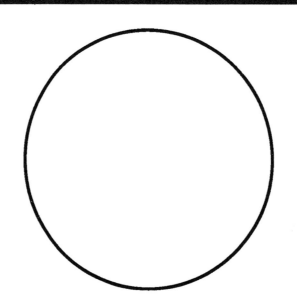

CHECKER–
CHECKS THE ASSIGNMENTS

USING COOPERATIVE SLOGANS

Three posters with cooperative slogans are found on the following pages. These posters may be reproduced or enlarged on colored paper and displayed on a bulletin board or around the classroom. All three may be displayed at the same time—or display them one at a time. The students themselves will be able to come up with many more slogans after beginning to use Cooperative Learning. Each group may even want to come up with a "Group Slogan" to display near its work space. This could be a slogan that helps to bring group members closer together, or to identify them as a team.

ROLE POSTERS

Four posters describing different group roles are found on pages 85 to 88. Reproduce these posters on differently-colored paper and display on a bulletin board to remind students of each role's responsibilities. See pages 73 to 80 for bulletin board ideas.

United We Stand, Divided We Fall

— GEORGE POPE MORRIS —

83

RECORDER

The **RECORDER** writes the cooperative group's answers on the paper. The **RECORDER** must make sure all members agree with the answers.

CHECKER

The CHECKER checks all work done by the group. The CHECKER also checks to make certain that ALL group members understand the assignment.

RUNNER

The RUNNER asks the teacher for help when no one else in the group can give an answer.

ENCOURAGER

The ENCOURAGER helps keep the group working together. The ENCOURAGER tells the group members when they are doing a good COOPERATIVE JOB!

COOPERATIVE LEARNING
TEACHING AIDS

STUDENT REWARDS

CERTIFICATES

Several certificates are found on pages 90–93. These certificates congratulate a student for successfully using cooperative skills. These certificates may be reproduced and used at any time, especially during the "practice" phase of cooperative skills development. If the certificate allows the student to receive an award, choose something you know the student would desire, or choose from the following list:

- Chew gum for the class period or the day
- A "no homework" pass
- Drop lowest grade this grading period
- Free time on the computer
- Bring money to buy a soft drink from the machines at the end of the day
- Free ice cream at lunch
- Free "100" on a homework assignment
- Trip to the gym or outside
- Free pencils, erasers, etc.
- Special field trip privilege
- Goody Box: Ask merchants in your neighborhood to donate inexpensive merchandise to use for rewards

PASSPORT

A passport is another way to earn rewards for demonstrating good cooperative skills. Reproduce the form on page 94. Write the student's name on the form and glue the form to a large index card. These cards should be stored in a file box, organized according to class period or subject. As students come into the class, they should pick up their cards. The teacher announces which cooperative skill will be practiced each day. As the teacher observes a student demonstrating the skill, a hole will be punched in one of the spaces on the card. When a student has all of the spaces punched, the card may be redeemed for a reward.

Because you,

used a quiet voice today,
you are entitled to

_____

_____

_____

Signed _____

I'm not
a BIG MOUTH

Because you,

used a quiet voice today,
you are entitled to

_____

_____

_____

Signed _____

I'm not
a BIG MOUTH

COOPERATION IS EVERYBODY'S JOB

AWARD

Presented To _____ for

_____

Signature _____

COOPERATION IS EVERYBODY'S JOB

AWARD

Presented To _____ for

_____

Signature _____

STUDENT'S NAME: _____

has been a Good Friend by

☆ explaining answers   ☆ expressing support

☆ asking probing questions ☆ listening

☆ criticizing ideas; not people ☆ expressing feelings

☆ summarizing   ☆ giving directions

☆ using a quiet voice

STUDENT'S NAME _____

You really hit a homerun with your cooperative skills !

COOPERATION 19
COMPETITION 4

TEACHER'S SIGNATURE _____

_____
STUDENT

has earned

an ice cream treat

for demonstrating

good cooperative skills

AUTHORIZED BY:_____

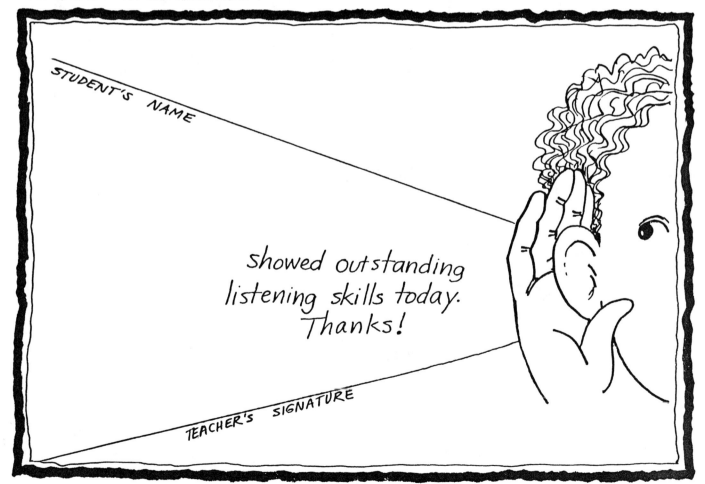

STUDENT'S NAME

showed outstanding
listening skills today.
Thanks!

TEACHER'S SIGNATURE

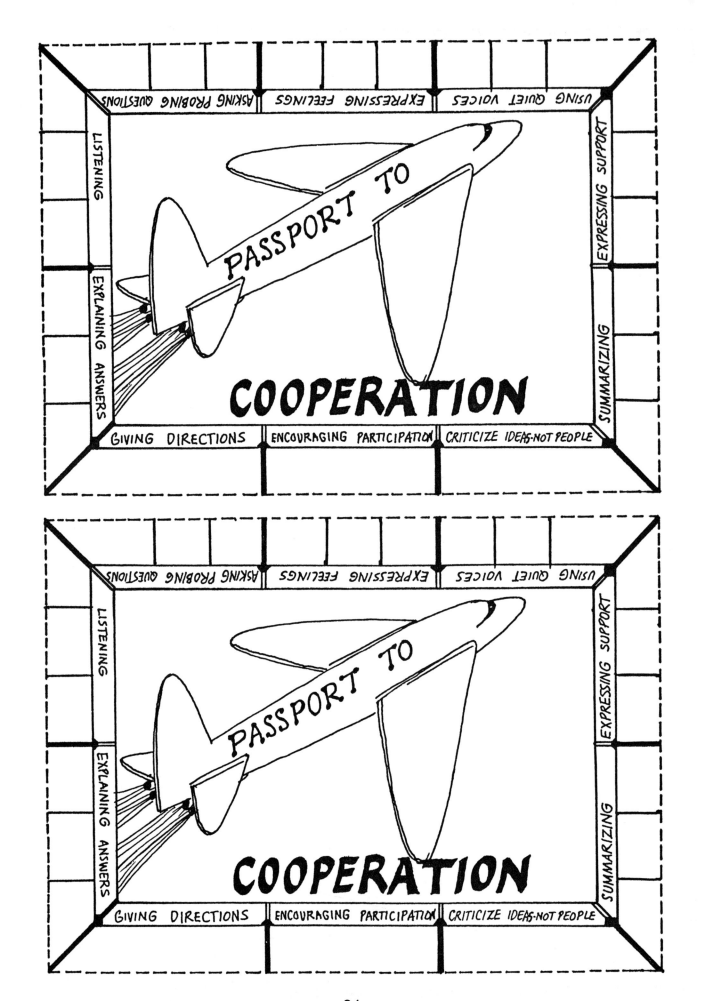

94

REFERENCES AND FURTHER READING

Breeden, T. & Mosley, J. *The Middle Grades Teacher's Handbook For Cooperative Learning.* Nashville, TN: Incentive Publications, 1991.

College Board. *Algebridge.* Providence, RI: Janson Publication, 1990.

Forte, Imogene. *Cooperative Learning Teacher Timesavers.* Nashville, TN: Incentive Publications, 1992.

Forte, I. & Schurr, S. *The Cooperative Learning Guide & Planning Pak For Middle Grades.* Nashville, TN: Incentive Publications, 1992.

Forte, I. & MacKenzie, J. *The Cooperative Learning Guide & Planning Pak For Primary Grades.* Nashville, TN: Incentive Publications, 1992.

Forte, I. & MacKenzie, J. *Pulling Together For Cooperative Learning.* Nashville, TN: Incentive Publications, 1991.

Gordon, Thomas. *Teacher Effectiveness Training.* New York, NY: Longman, Inc., 1974.

Hill, S. & Hill, T. *The Collaborative Classroom.* Portsmouth, NH: Heinemann, 1990.

Hyde, A. & Hyde, P. *Mathwise.* Portsmouth, NH: Heinemann, 1991.

Johnson, R. & Johnson, D. *Warm-Ups, Grouping Strategies, and Group Activities.* Edina, MN: Interaction Book, 1990.

Johnson, Johnson, & Holubec. *Structuring Cooperative Learning.* Edina, MN: Interaction Book Co., 1987.

Johnson, R. & Johnson, D. *Advanced Cooperative Learning.* Edina, MN: Interaction Book Co., 1988.

Johnson, R. & Johnson, D. *Circles of Learning (Third Edition).* Edina, MN: Interaction Book Co., 1990.

Kagan, S. *Cooperative Learning Resources for Teachers.* Riverside, CA: Resources For Teachers, 1989.

Sebranek, Meyer, & Kemper. *Write Source 2000.* Burlington, WI: The Write Source Publishing House, 1990.